"Clever and colorful, *How To Be an Urban Cowgirl & Find Your Inner West* makes a charming gift for the adventurous woman who is cowgirl curious and ready to ride the range. Saddle up and discover the style, the attitude, and unlimited vistas in unleashing your own true inner West."

–ELLEN BYERRUM, author of *The Crime of Fashion Mysteries*

"A lively little guide that brings the West right to your doorstep and a joyful ride from cover to cover. It's fun, friendly, and impossible not to smile."

–ROWDY OLSON, partner and marketing manager at *Western Trading Post*

"From hats to horses and from pickup lines to cooking over a campfire, Corinne Joy Browns guide to everything cowgirl is quick, fun, and a fact-filled read for anyone who wants to know the difference between an Urban Cowgirl and Ranch Cowgirl. Browns breezy and sometimes irreverent writing style serves her well in capturing the essence of the Western way of life."

–JOANNE DAVIDSON, former editor at *Denver Post Society*, contributing writer at *Colorado Politics* and *Denver Gazette*.

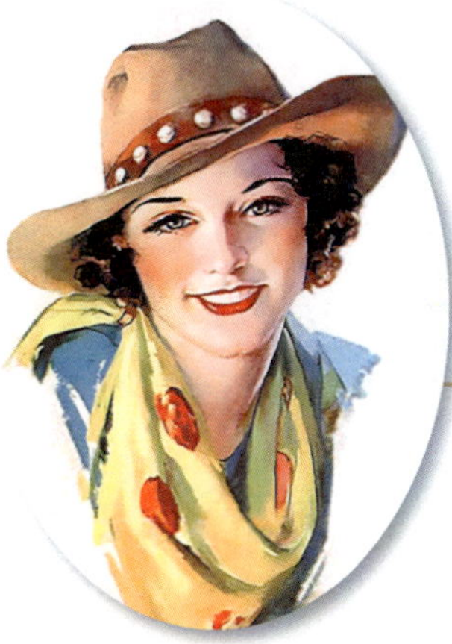

HOW TO BE AN URBAN COWGIRL
& FIND YOUR INNER WEST

By Corinne Joy Brown

SPRING CEDARS®

With thanks to all the cowgirls who have inspired me and all the women who have shared in celebrating the cowgirl way of life. And a very special hat-tip to graphic designer Ling Sigstedt for helping realize my vision.

First edition, 2026

Page 10: Maidenform bra – courtesy of Hanes Brands Inc.
Page 17: concho belt – courtesy of Alltribes Indian Art
Page 18: fringe wrap skirt – courtesy of Pat Dahnke
Page 27: – courtesy of Rockmount Ranch Wear
Book design by Ling Sigstedt

ISBN 978-1-963117-83-7 (hardback)

Published by Spring Cedars
Denver, Colorado
www.springcedars.com

CHAPTERS

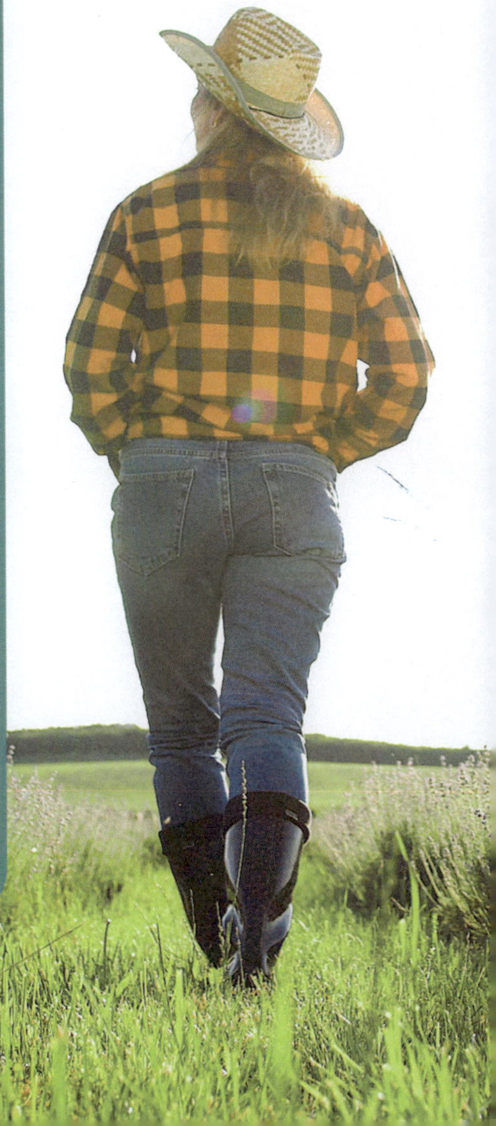

CHAPTER 1

A Sense of Place

Do you dream about wide open spaces?

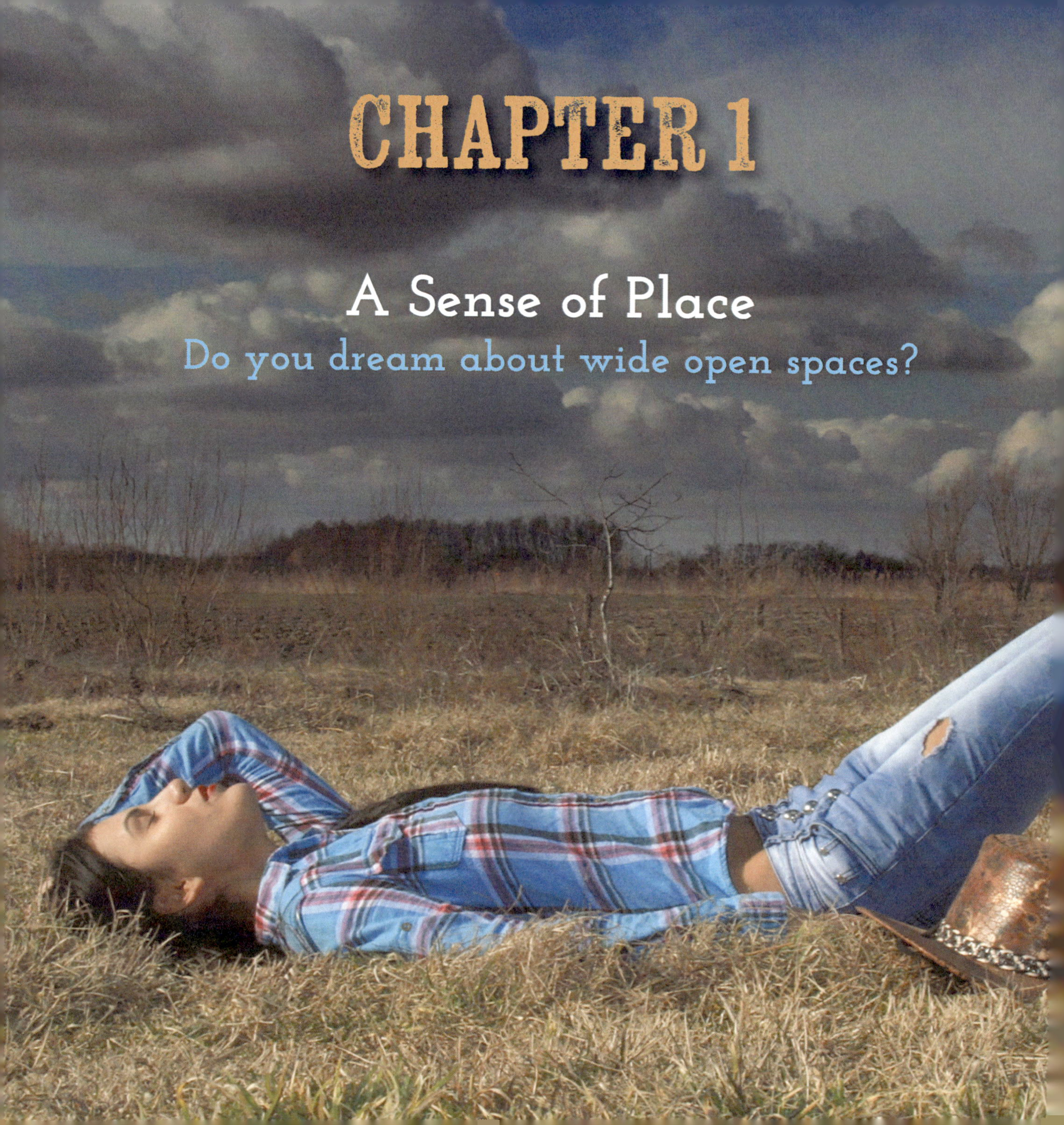

Wish you had a horse instead
of a canary?

Wear cowboy boots
to the office?

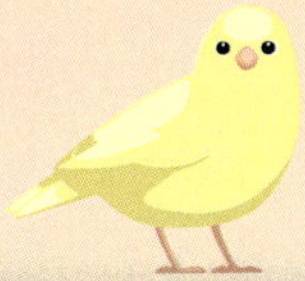

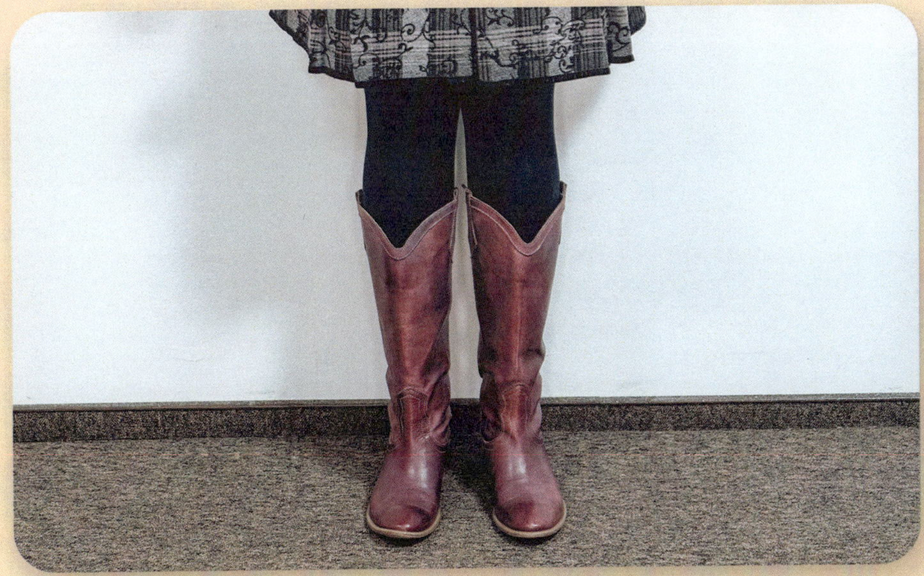

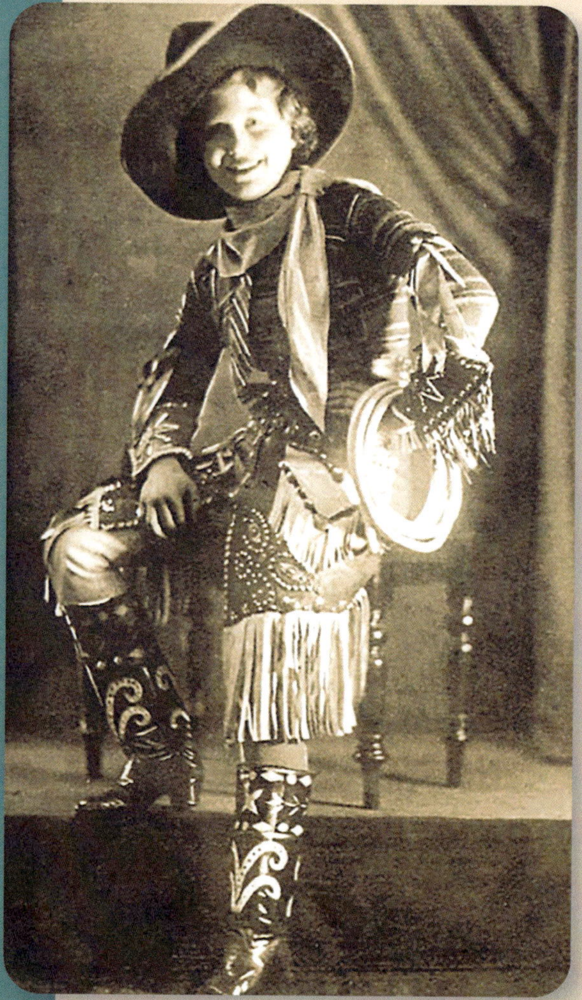

You're an urban cowgirl, and we can help.

Follow this guide to the cowgirl life: urban solutions to cowgirl fashion, fitness, pop culture, and food.

Discover your inner West!

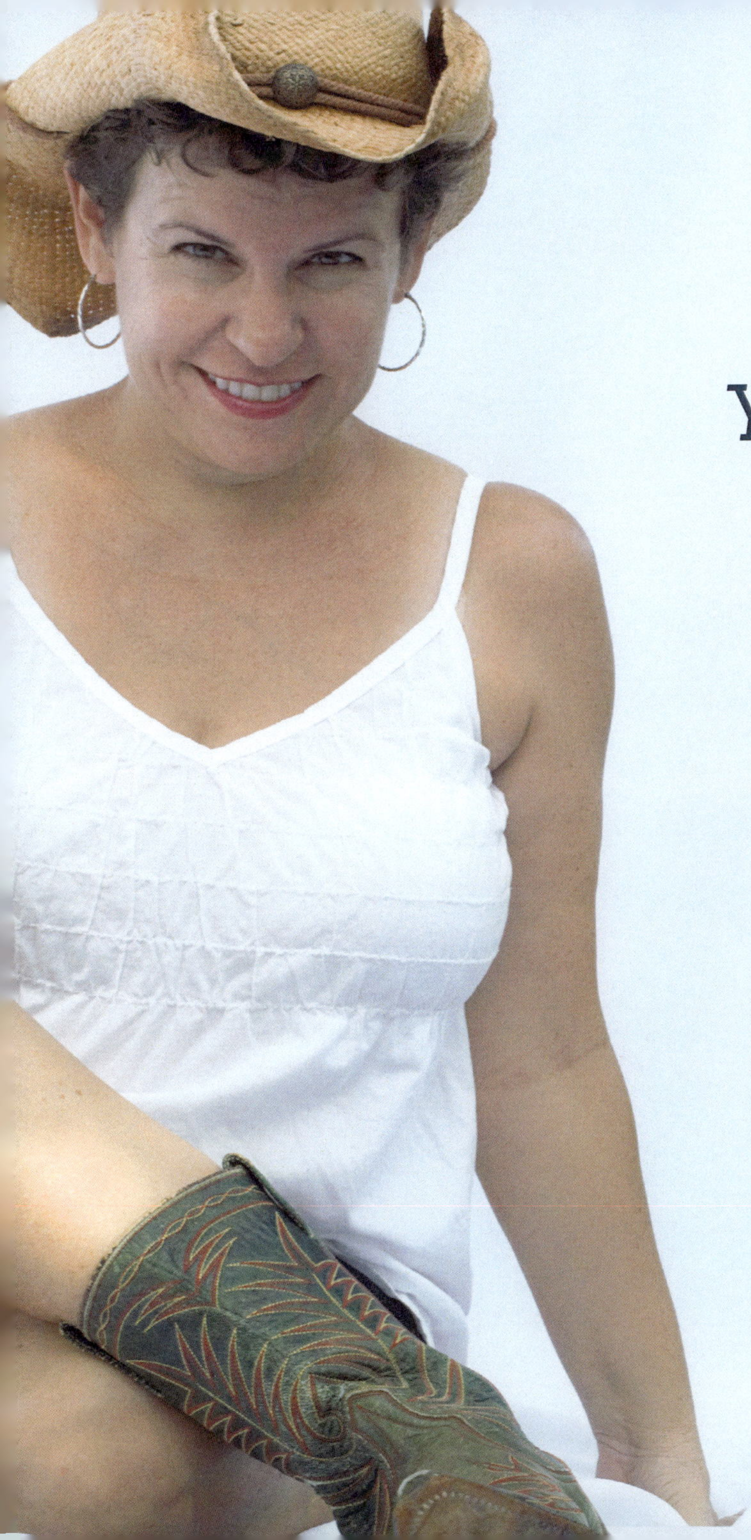

You know who you are...

CHAPTER 2

Home, Home on the Range

Where you live doesn't matter.

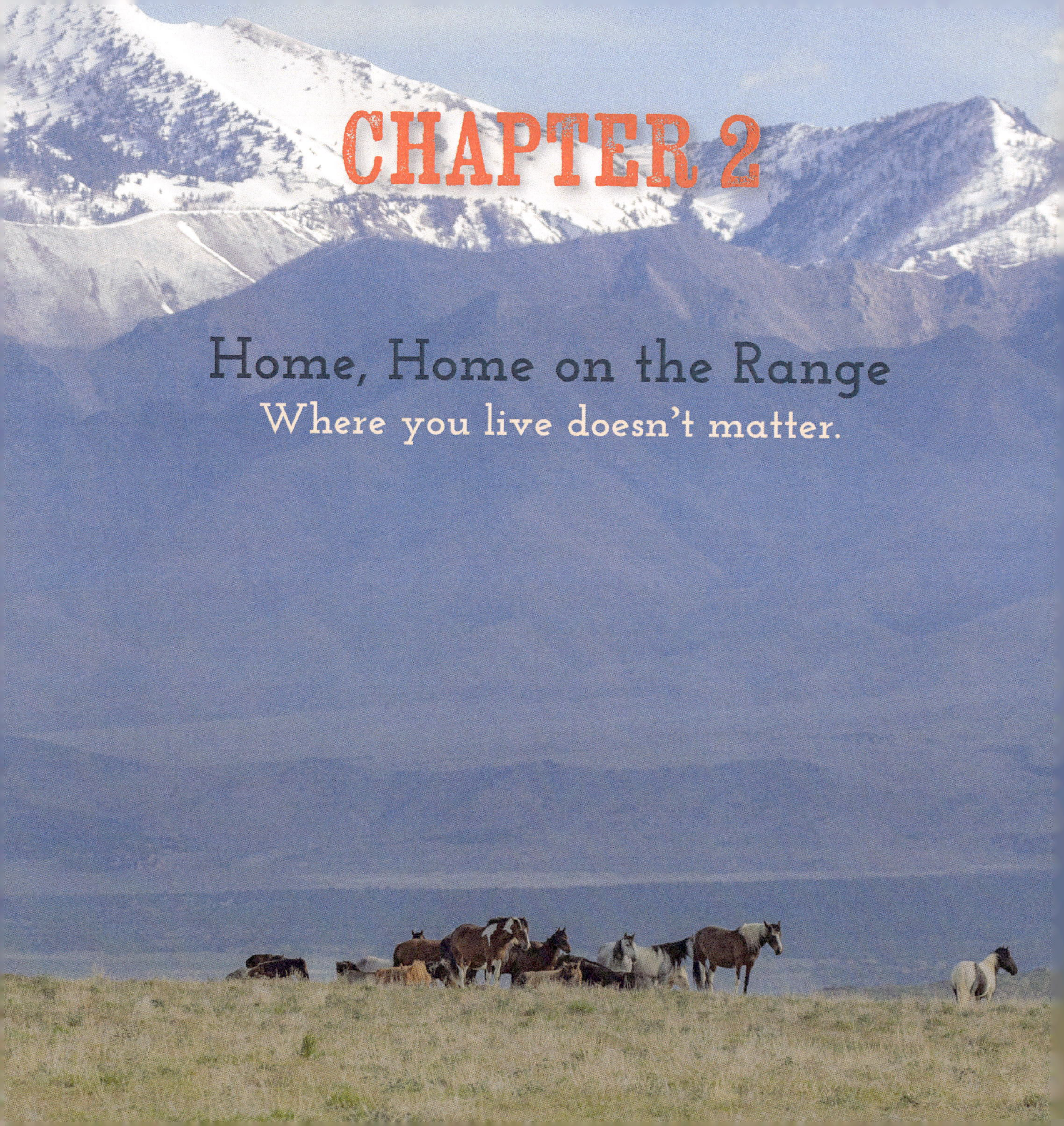

Apartment, house, condo, or trailer, it's all the same.
The range is wherever you are.

Hang a picture of a sunset on your living room wall.
Ride into it every chance you get.

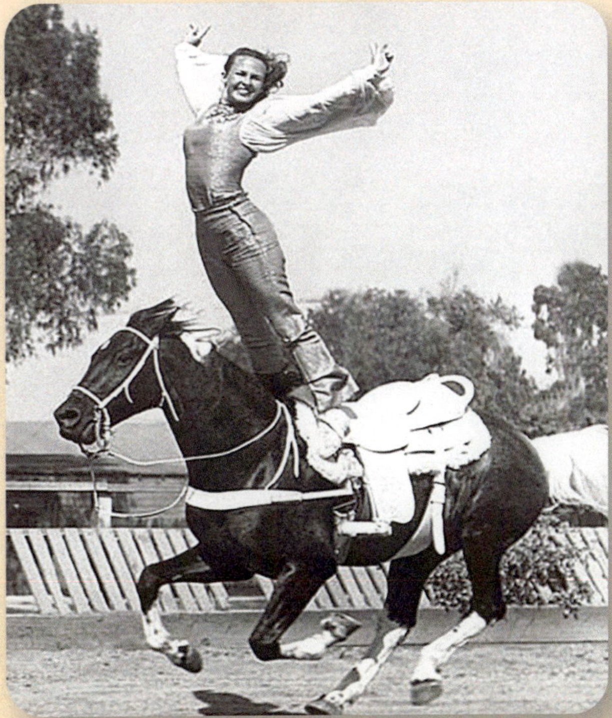

CHAPTER 3

Owning a Horse

Owning a horse is unnecessary.

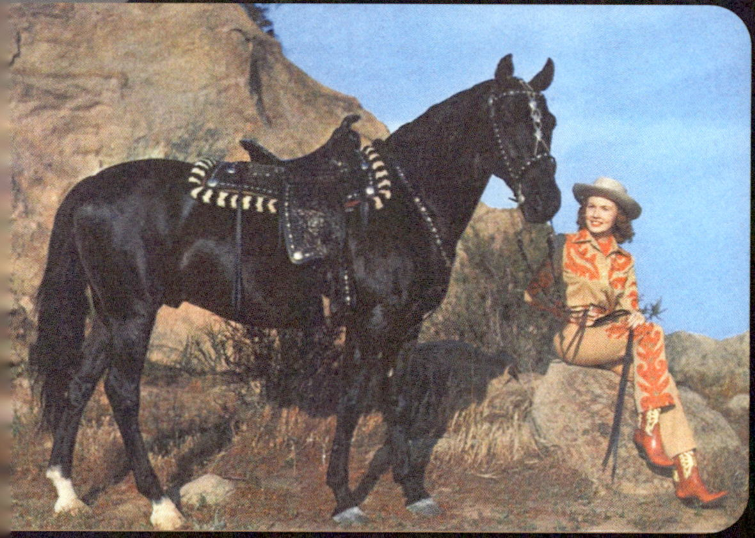

Any dog, cat, reptile, fish, or feathered thing will do. Name it Tex, Rex, Red, or any other cowboy-sounding term you like. No one will know the difference.

Get the bumper sticker:
"My other ride is a purebred Appaloosa."

But if you have a horse, all the better.
You're practically the real deal.

Most urban cowgirls with horses usually ride on weekends. It's an expensive hobby. Their horses are often pampered, spoiled and replace boyfriends. In some cases, the horses have their own personal trainer. If you don't have one, you can join a gym instead and get a trainer of your own. But if you insist on purchasing an equine, consider black. They go with whatever you're wearing.

CHAPTER 4

The Outfit

There's a cowgirl lurking in your closet.

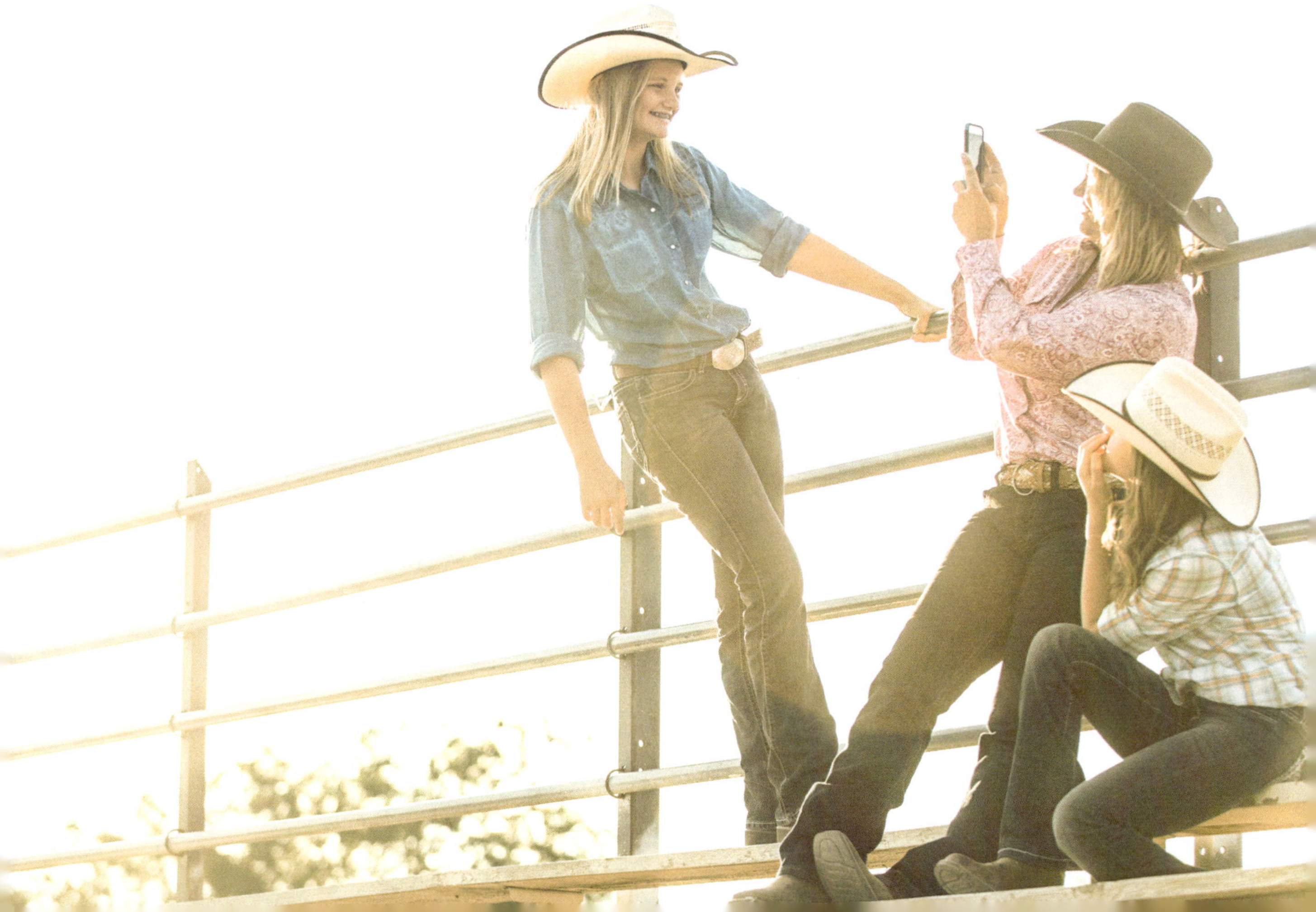

Let her out every chance you get. From your Spanx to your Spandex, it's about attitude!

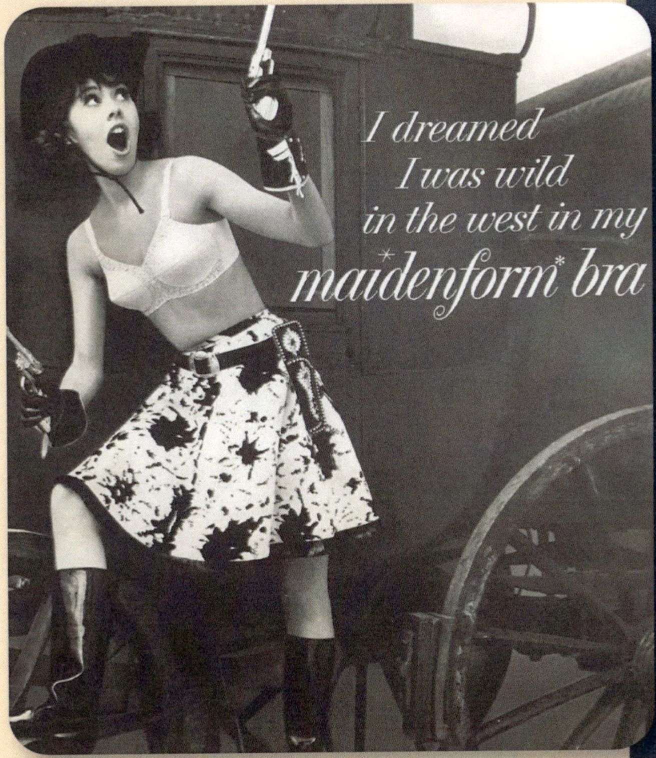

Start with stretch or boot-cut jeans. These can be indigo, faded, or shredded. Add a long-sleeved shirt: plaid, striped, or floral. White is always nice. Snaps are *essential*. A tank top also works well. Add a denim jacket. Very, very nice.

You can go Vintage, Bo-Ho, or Retro-Rock. Today's cowgirls come in several styles and sizes. Beyond the basics in ranch dressing, (and we're not talking salad here), you have miles to go.

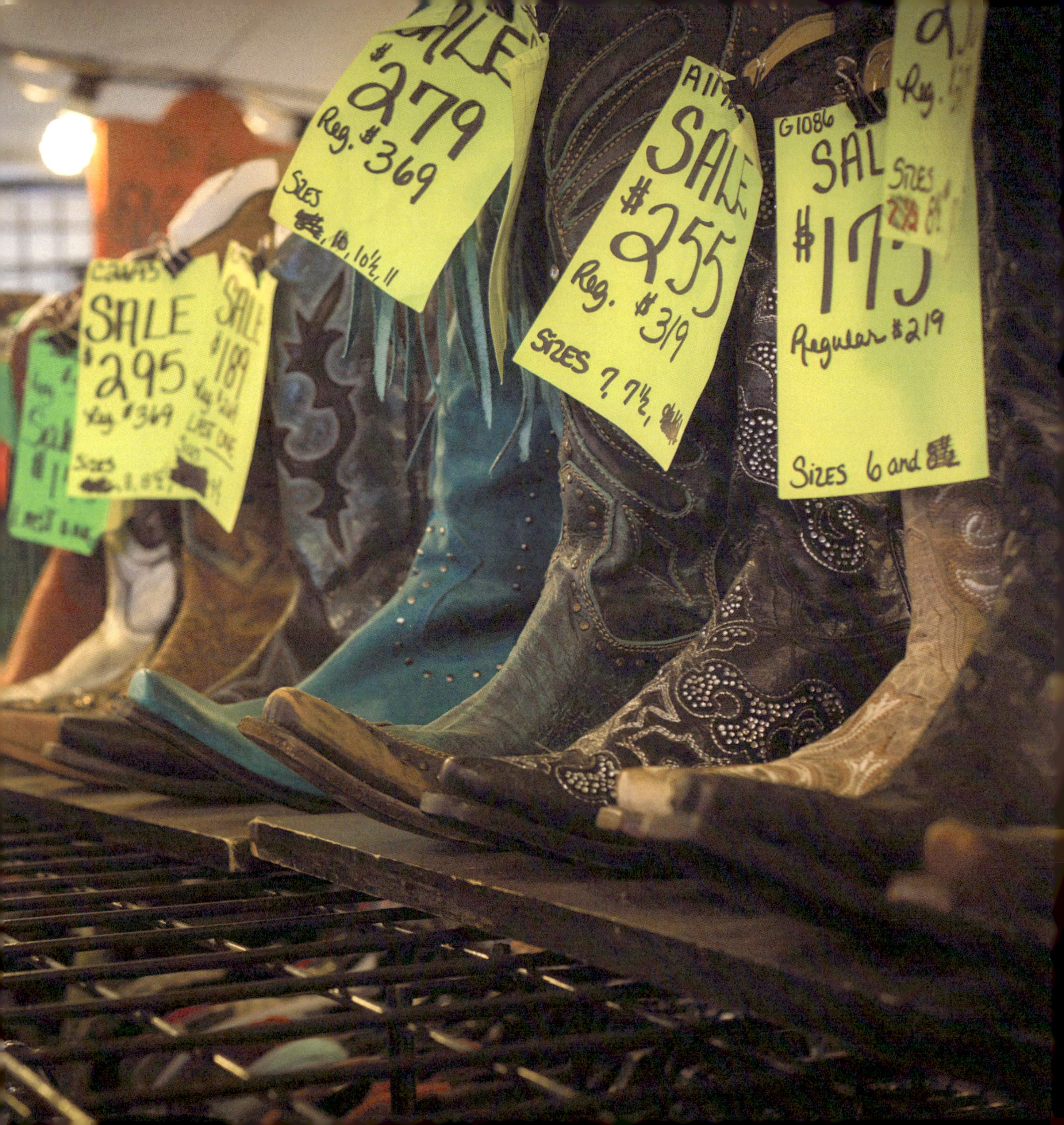
SALE
$279
Reg. $369
SALE
$255
Reg. $319
G1086
Regular $219
SALE
$295
Reg. $369

But first, where to find the goods and who makes 'em...

Retailers

Ranch Cowgirl	Urban Cowgirl
Cavender's	Nordstrom
Boot Barn	DSW Shoes
Murdoch's	TJ Maxx
Cowgirl Baroness	Dillard's

Brands

Ranch Cowgirl	Urban Cowgirl
Kimes Ranch Jeans	Democracy
Wrangler	Levis
Ariat	Ralph Lauren
Pat Dahnke	Lucky Brand

You can often get "the look" from stores you know and love. If not, head to the nearest Western boutique or ranch & feed store for the above brands and stock up.

CHAPTER 5

Wardrobe Particulars

Urban cowgirls get fancy.

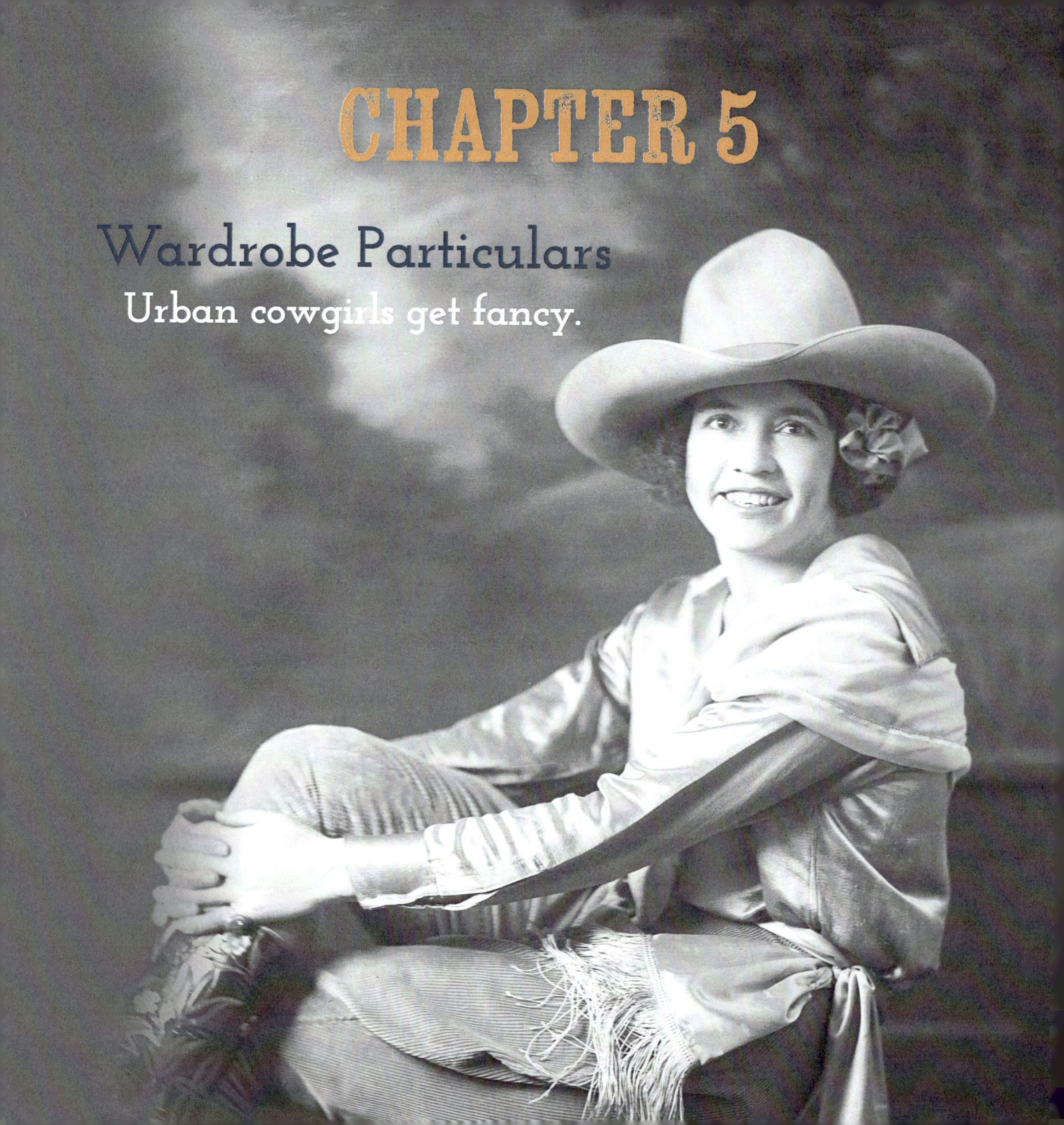

For a night out on the town, city gals have learned that leather, suede, and lace are okay. Short skirts are *always* okay. Turquoise jewelry is very okay. Flat, mid-heel, or high-heeled cowboy boots are acceptable everywhere, to be worn with *everything*.

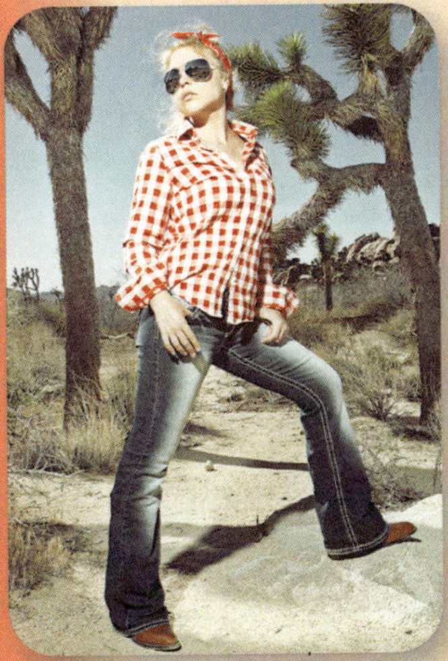

Snap-shirts, invented by Rockmount RanchWear, were made for a reason; to save a cowboy's life if a shirt gets caught by a steer's horn. Let's be honest—they're also very convenient. Saves time.

Jeans come in all shapes and sizes, but, like your favorite Starbucks, you need to know how to buy 'em: ***"Extra-long, light wash, sandblast, boot-cut, and high-rise."*** Be specific.

But beware: low-rise means hip hugger. Flared means bell-bottom. If you're old enough to remember those jeans, you're too old to wear 'em!

CHAPTER 6

Urban Cowgirl Essentials

The secret is in the accessories.

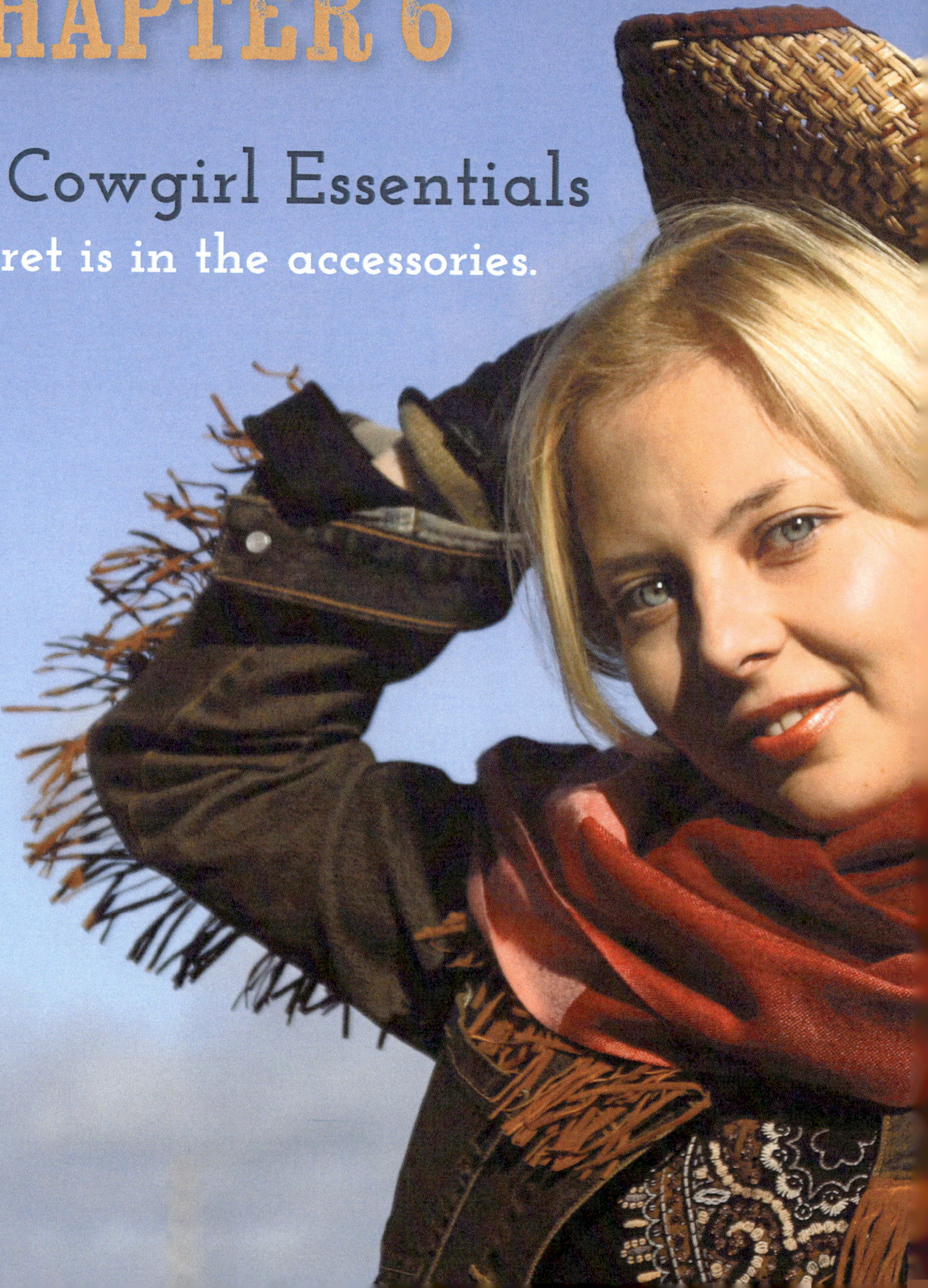

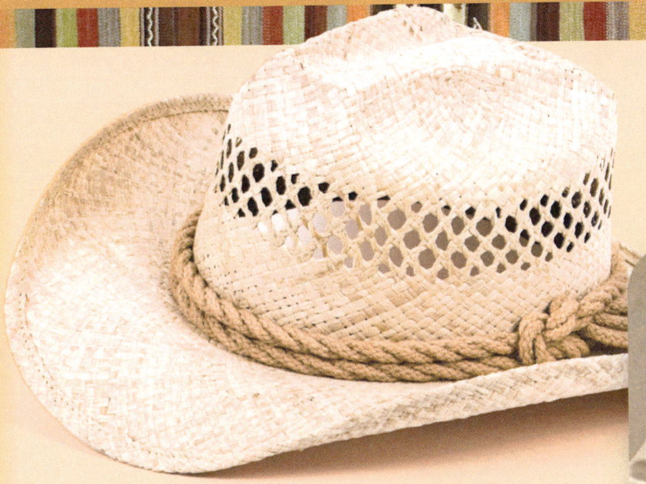

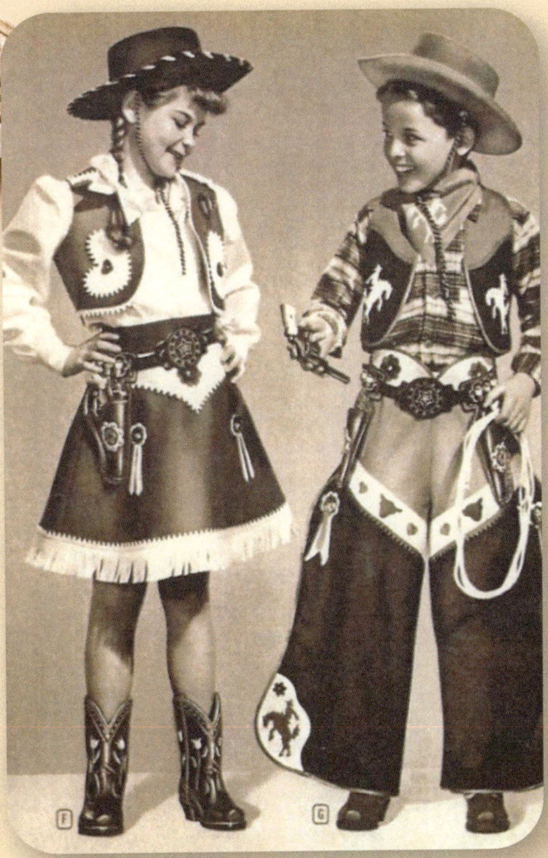

Hats- Straw, felt, or wool, hats are optional, unless you're headed for the rodeo. Always wear a hat to the rodeo.

Belts- Cinched around your waist, slung low on the hip, wide or narrow, a belt is never optional. A belt with bling is still acceptable, but silver conchos forever wrap you in style. Alltribes' frontier classic!

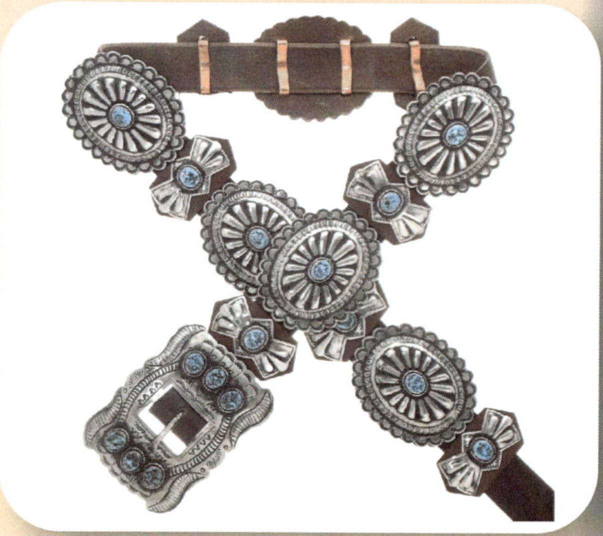

Boots- Ranch cowgirls wear Roper, Shyanne, and Idyllwind boots. Urban cowgirls wear Steve Madden, Matisse, and Tres Outlaws. Cowboy boots can be worn to work, the barn, and out-on-the-town!

Buckles- Buckles are like little billboards and the bigger the better. You can find them used online. Rodeo buckles tell a story; try to find the buckle that tells yours!

Fringe- You simply cannot have too much fringe. Jackets, skirts, handbags, belts, and boots. Ask Texas designer Pat Dahnke. Fringe never goes out of style.

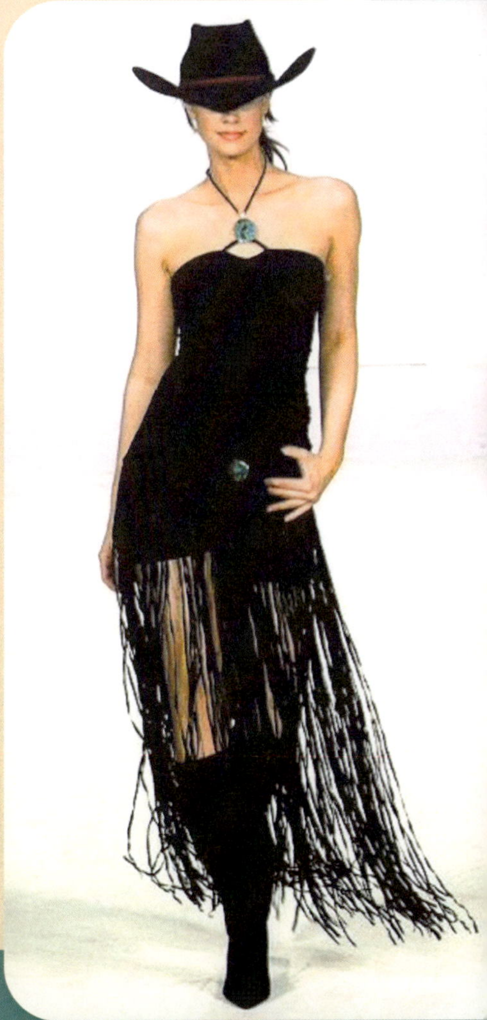

The Bandana or Wild Rag- Real cowgirls use these for everything: dust, wind, snot, decoration, even cleaning their tack.

Urban cowgirls use them on their dogs.

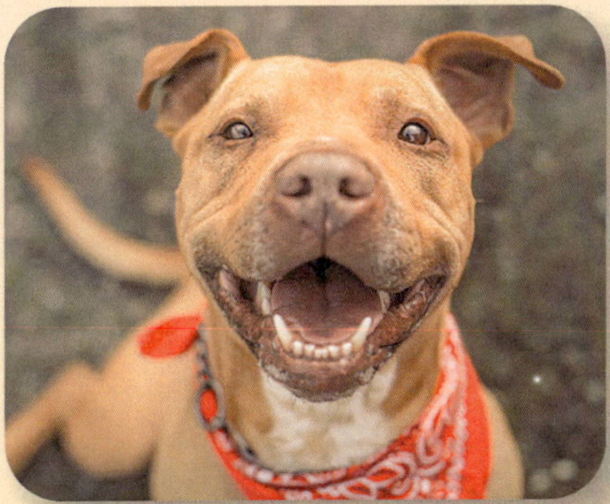

About boots: Okay ladies: Here's the long and short of it. Boots are useful for strolling, riding, and stomping your feet on the dance floor!

When you shop for boots you can ask for booties (ankle height), peewees (above the ankle), mid-calf (below the knee), and knee high! If that's not enough, you can get them embellished, tooled, quilted, overlaid, underlaid, lined, unlined, laced, zippered, embroidered, and studded.

You can have a high heel, an underslung heel, a flat heel, or a walking heel. Choose from a snip toe, a pointed toe, a square toe, or a rounded one. Best of all, you can wear them with jeans, shorts, skirts and dresses, or—***nothing at all!***

Real cowgirls rely on boots to protect their feet from hooves and dirt, stay in the saddle, and get the job done.

Urban cowgirls wear boots because they look good.

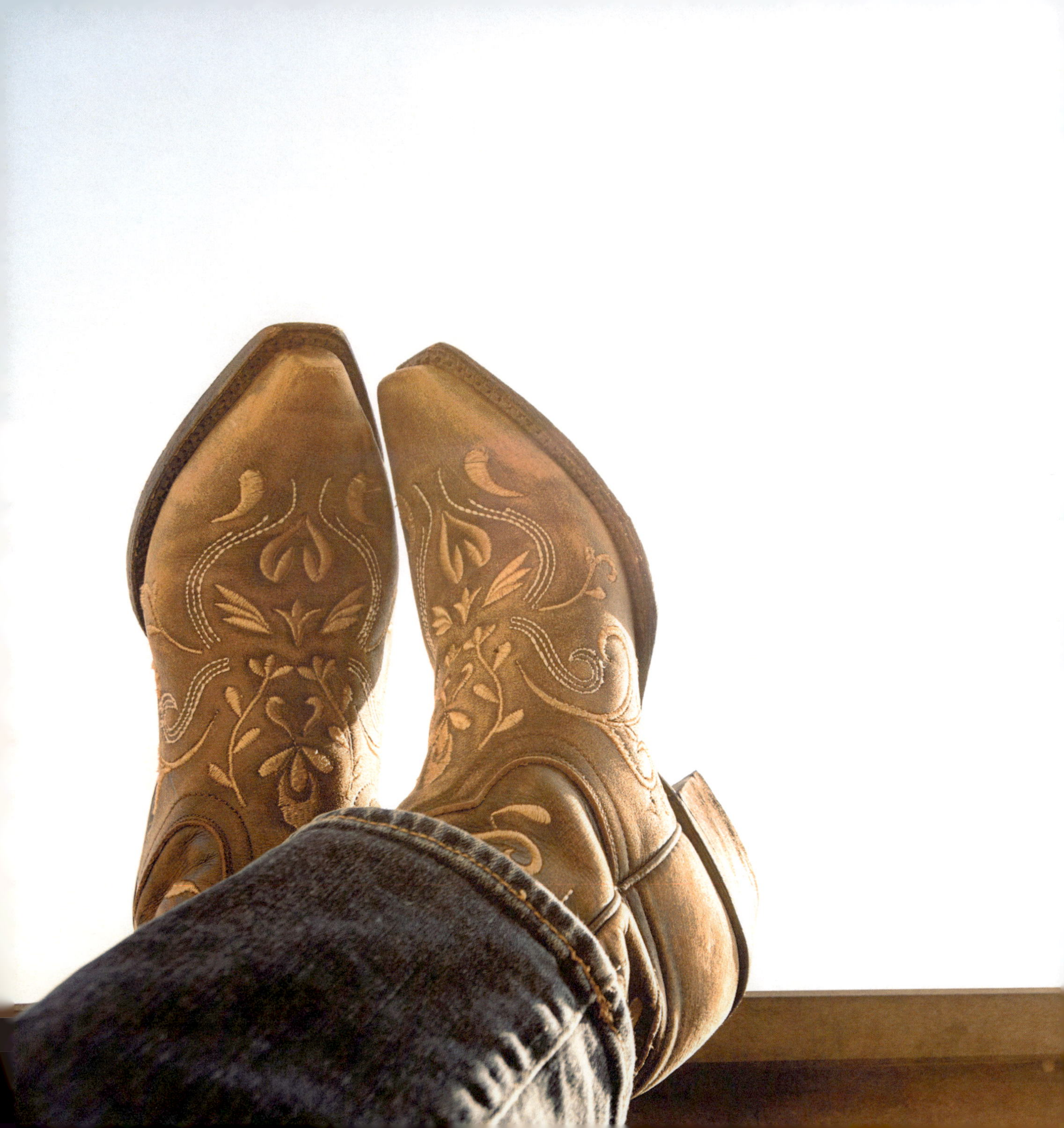

CHAPTER 7

Personal Accessories

Key to an urban cowgirl.

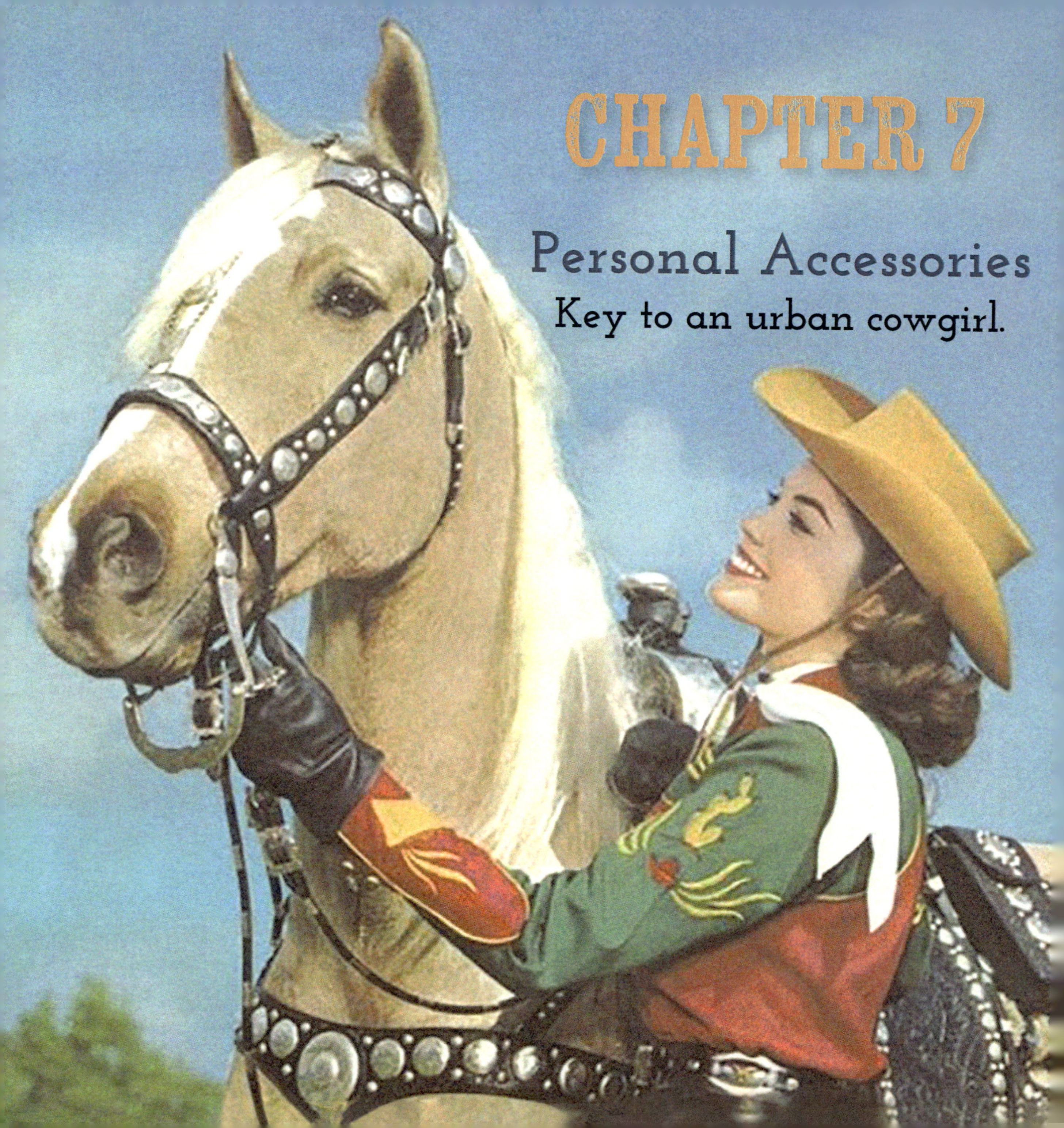

Even if you're not wearing Western garb, all anyone has to do is look closely to learn the truth: It's in the details.

Urban Cowgirl Purse	Ranch Cowgirl Purse
Hand cream	Bag balm
Cologne	DEET
Keychain	Hoof pick
Nail polish-Summer Pink	Barn Red
Cell phone tone-Chris Stapleton	Horse whinny

Urban Cowgirl Car	Ranch Cowgirl Car
Sports version-Triumph	Mustang
Mid-size-Hundai	Jeep Wrangler
SUV-Range Rover	Chevy Silverado
Convertible	Ford Bronco

Urban Sleepwear	Ranch Sleepwear
Flannel jammies	BVDs
Short nightie	John Deere t-shirt & boxers

CHAPTER 8

The Rodeo

A rodeo is an urban cowgirl's Super Bowl.

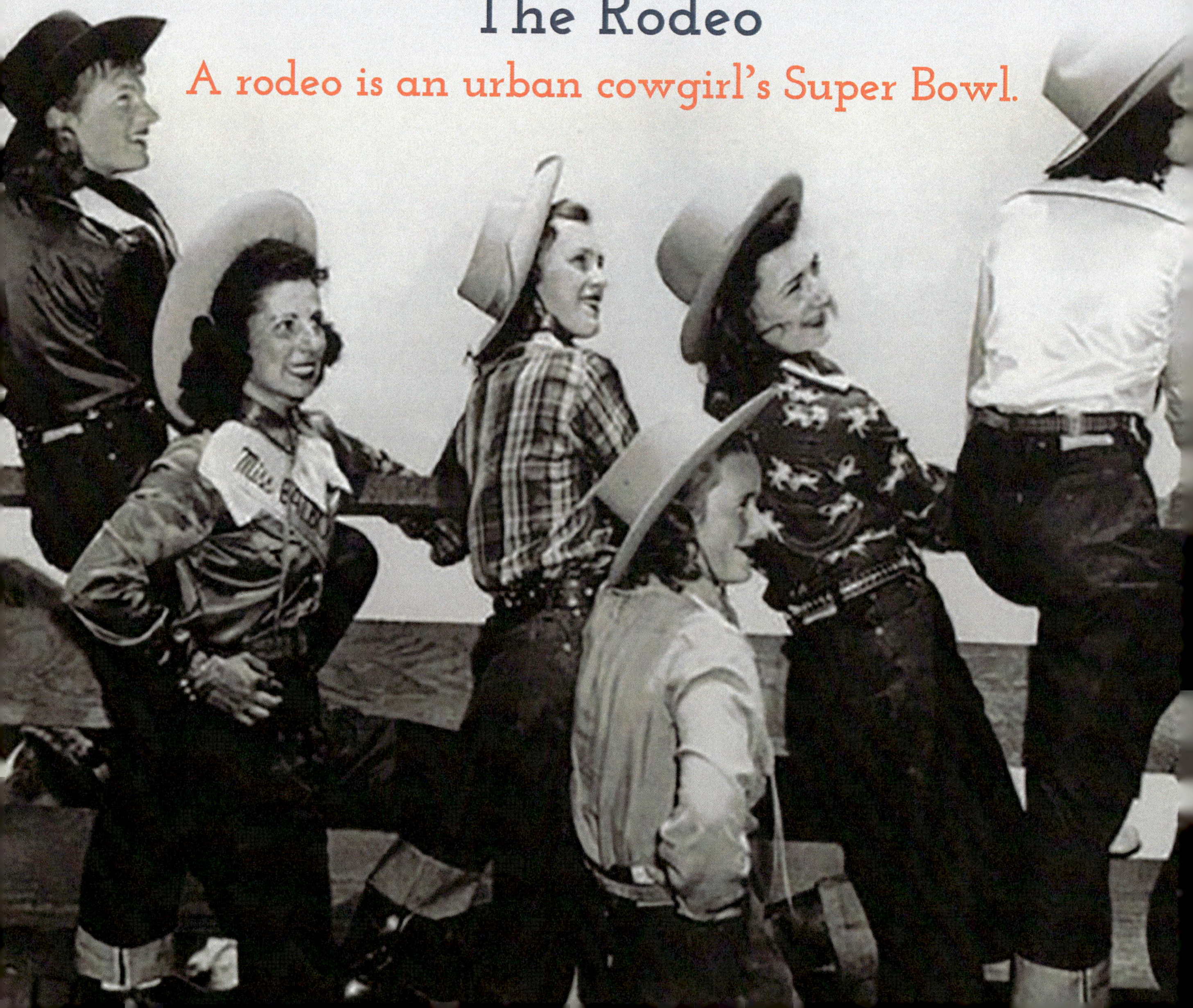

Go local, the NFR or Cheyenne Frontier Days.

Attend with your friends; it's twice as much fun. Rodeos are the best place to see real live action! Here you can watch cowboys ride broncs and cowgirls rope, ride, and barrel race. But be careful what you say; terminology counts!

Rodeo Terms:

Rodeo Queen- Mostly still She/Her/Hers

Pickup Men- Not what you think.

Eight Seconds- A good ride... anytime.

Flank Strap- Used to make a horse buck.

Flankman- Definitely not what you think.

Rough Stock- Horses raised for bronc riding. They're rank, mean, and ornery. Not your grocery store pony.

Chute- Where it all starts. Keep your eyes on the gate!

Bulldogging- A man, a horse, and a bull; pure testosterone and guts.

Hazer- A guy on another horse that stays alongside the bull to keep it running straight, so the other cowboy can jump on it, grab it by the horns, and wrestle it to the ground. (Or, as my mother used to say, "You call this a living?")

Tie-down- Also not what you think.

Piggin' string- Picture this: Dash into an arena after a running calf, rope the calf, leap off your horse, throw the animal down, and wrap three legs—generally a front one and the two back ones—with a piggin' string, usually leather. Now you know.

Hooey- Far from nonsense, this is the knot used to tie the calf's three legs.

Cowboy Up!- This could have several meanings depending on the situation.

There's more—just take it one step at a time.

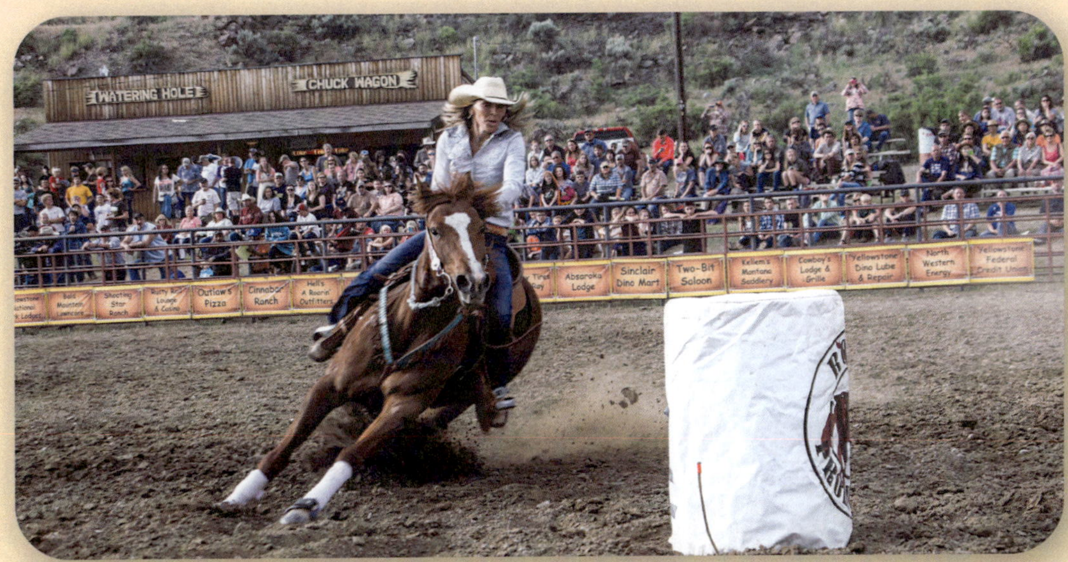

CHAPTER 9

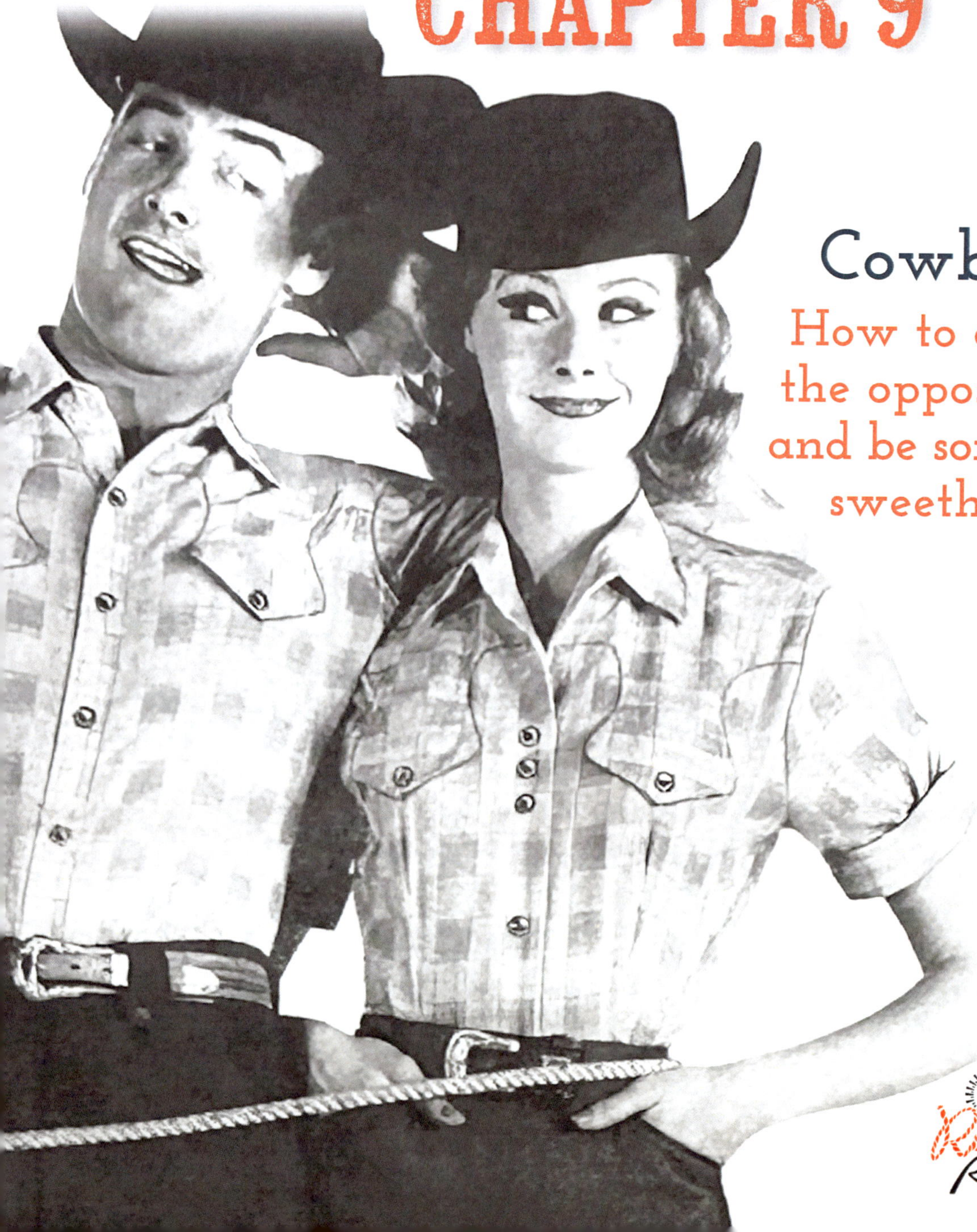

Cowboys

How to attract the opposite sex and be someone's sweetheart.

Looking for love? Romance is the same no matter who or where you are. Real cowboys enjoy charm, wit, humor, and cleavage. They have big hearts, are loyal and vulnerable, and also, hard to find.

To catch a cowboy, consider trading in your Hyundai for a 4x4. That should break the ice. Otherwise, a nice smile always helps. Then again, should you happen to meet a real cowboy, we recommend a few proven opening lines like:

"I see by your outfit..."

"Leave your horse outside?"

"Nice boots..."

"Is that your brand?"(referring to his tattoo)

"Got a little room in this saddle for two?"

Then there's the issue of competition.

A wise man once said, "The difference between western music and country music goes like this: In western music, a cowboy is in love with his horse... in country music, a cowboy is in love with somebody else's horse!"

Our advice?

If you meet a cowboy, always carry a lump of sugar in your purse.

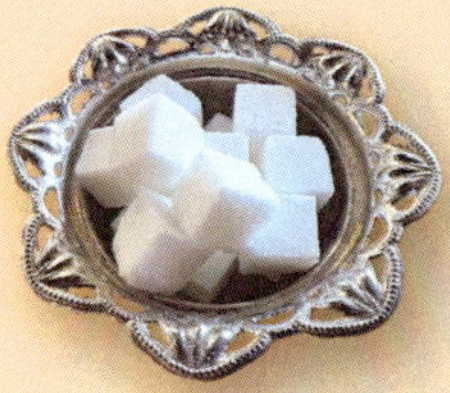

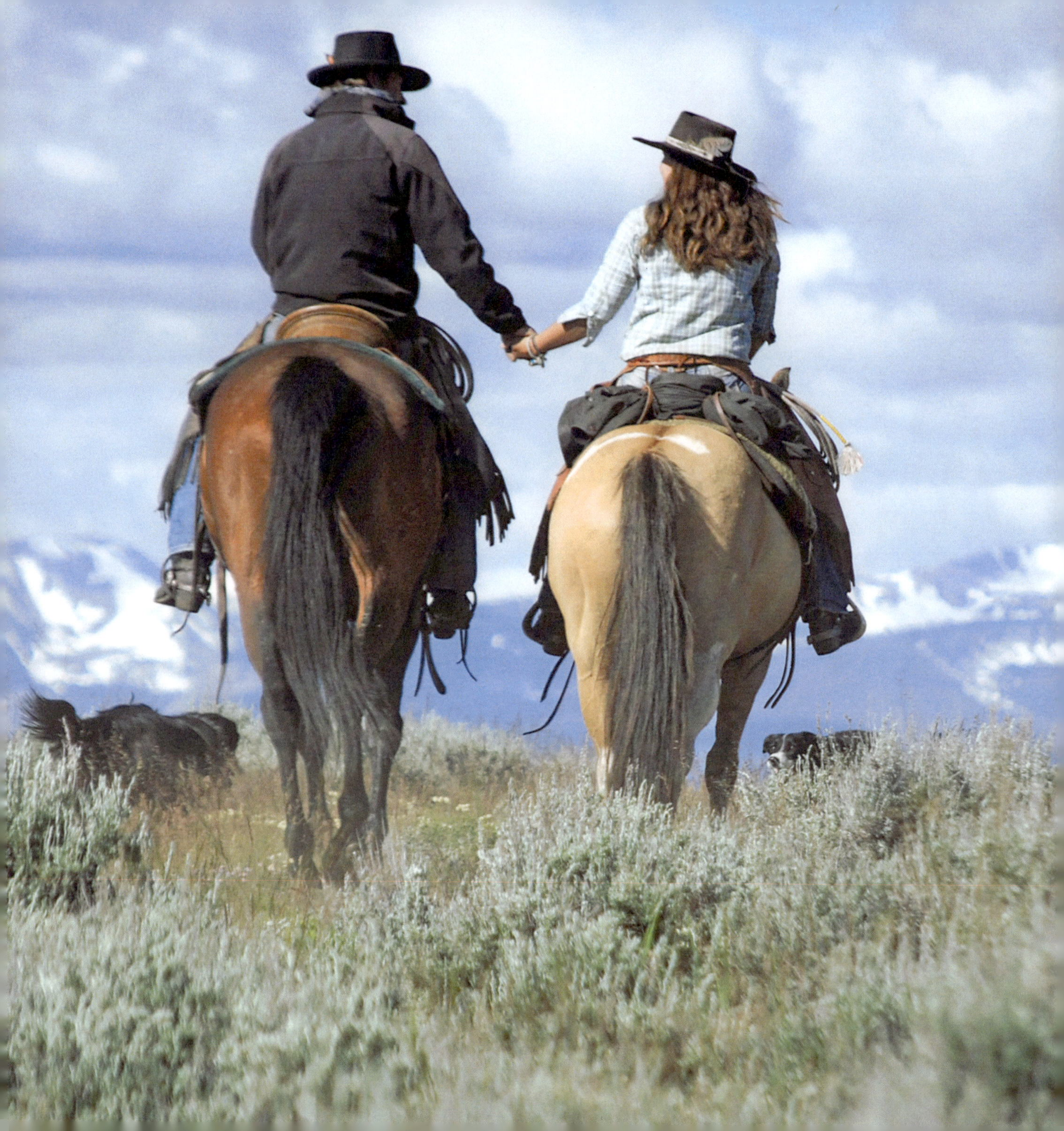

CHAPTER 10

Did Someone Say Dinner?

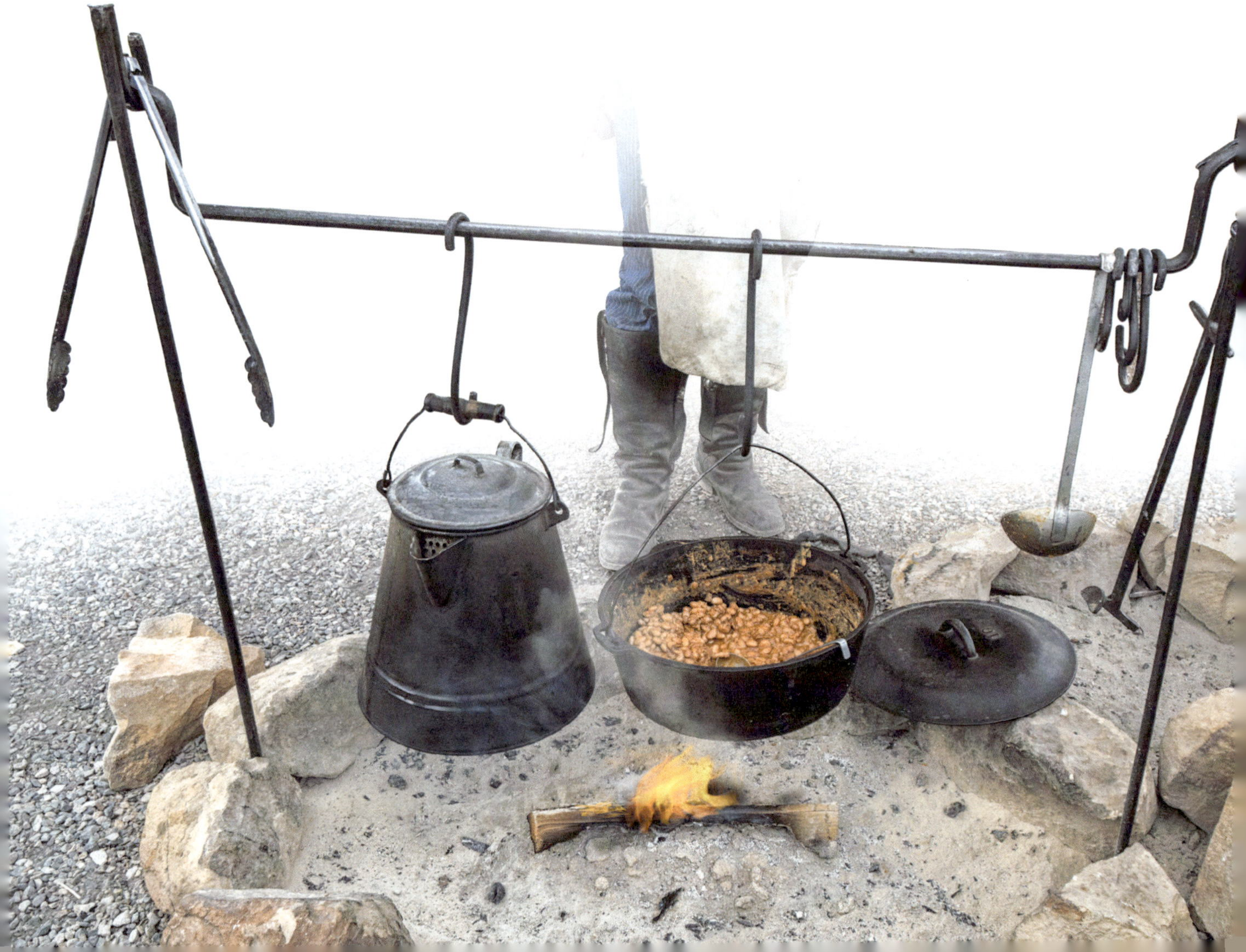

A real cowgirl knows how to cook over an open fire, on a barbecue, or on a grill. Ranch cooking is an acquired skill. It can involve cast iron, a lot of lard, large portions called "man-size", something called a cobbler, usually peach, and time. Plus coffee, always black.

Western cooking started out on the range. Meals were assembled on the back of a chuckwagon, a kind of rolling kitchen, like a food truck.

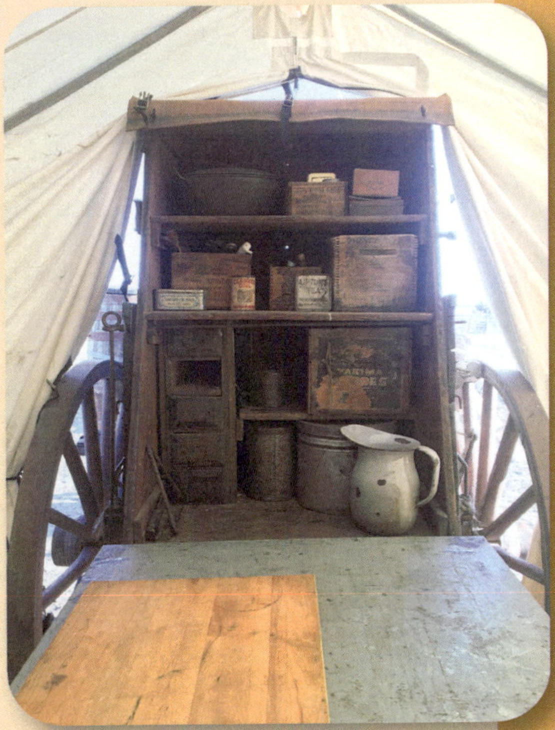

Basic ingredients included beef, potatoes, and beans. Breakfast and dinner had to stick to your ribs all day long. No cowboy ever heard of takeout or DoorDash

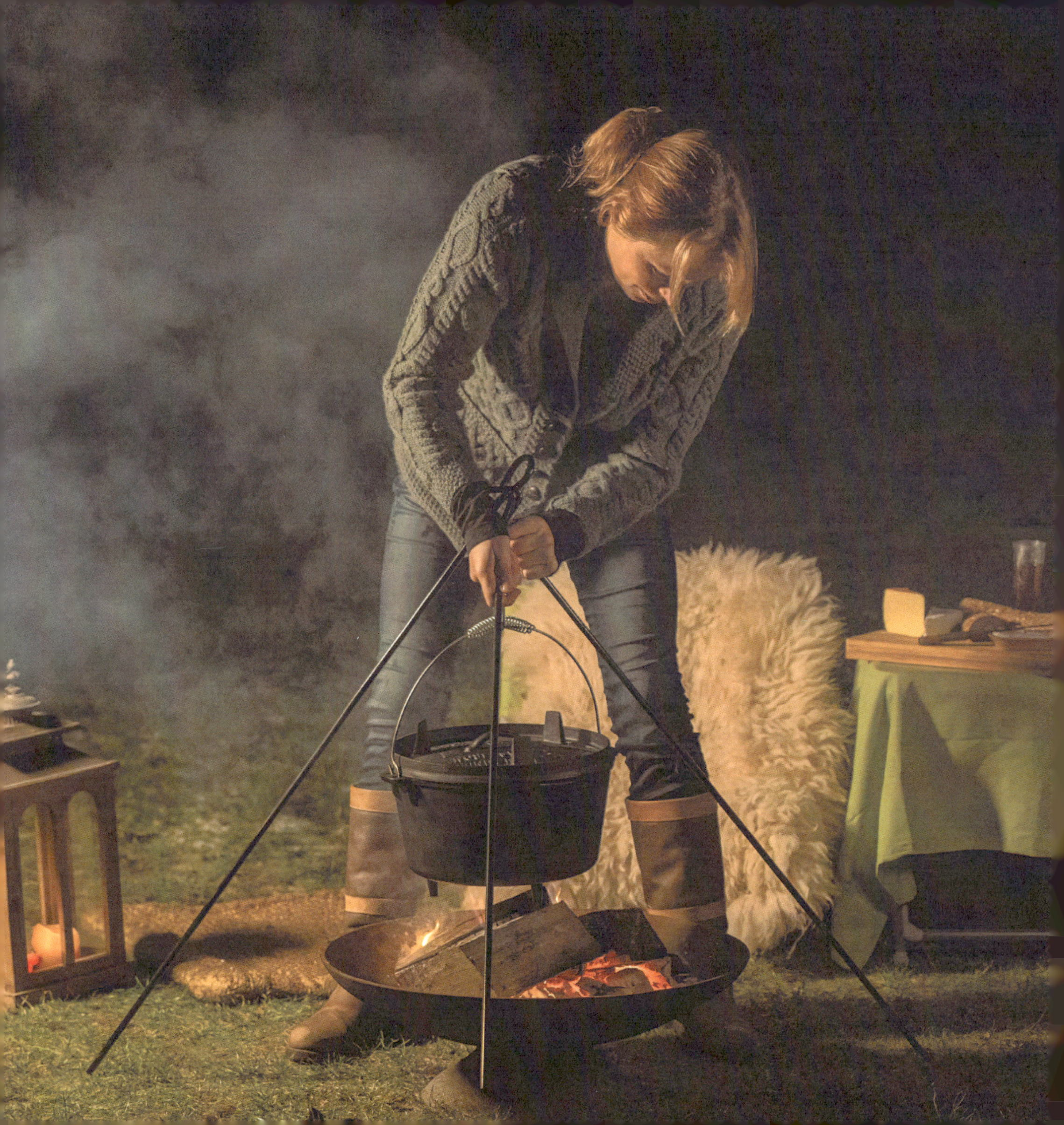

(They are not vegetarians.) But here's the good news:

You don't need a chuckwagon. Just stock up on Western tools and ingredients so your cowboy feels like he's at home.

For example:

Urban Cowgirl Kitchen	Ranch Cowgirl Kitchen
Sushi	Jerky
Pimento	Jalapeno
Ramen	Chili
Croissants	Cornbread
Focaccia	Biscuits
Chardonnay	Jack Daniels
Microwave	Dutch oven

You get the idea.

CHAPTER 11

Lifestyle and Staying Fit

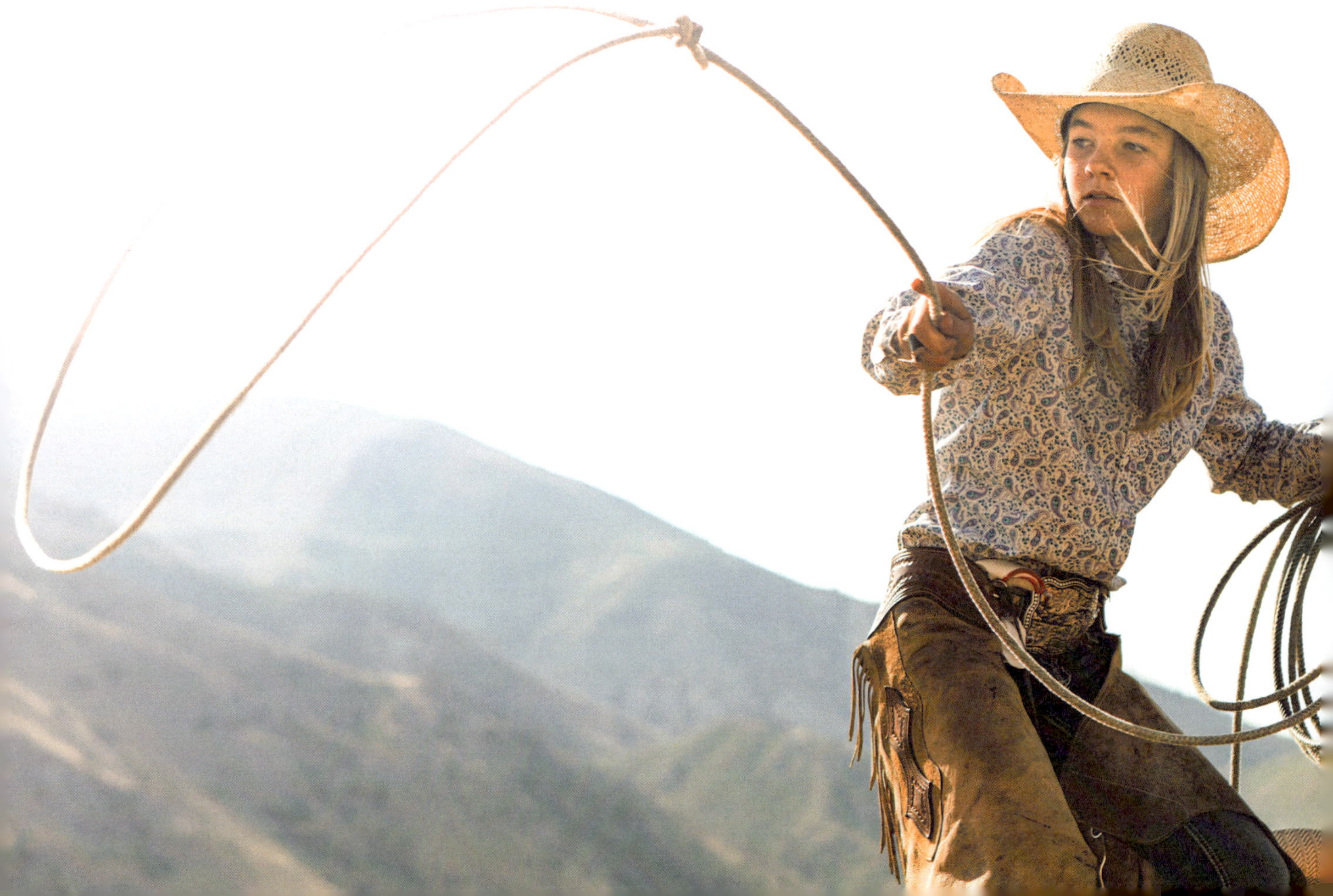

Ranch cowgirls stack hay, muck stalls, chop and haul wood, and groom animals. They raise kids, mend clothes, clean tack, hose trucks, fork straw, sweep barns, train horses, run barrels, rope calves, brand heifers, and herd steers.
Urban cowgirls line dance.

On the radio:
Ranch cowgirls like Dave Stamey, George Strait, Jason Aldean and Lainey Wilson.
Urban cowgirls listen to Keith Urban.

On vacation:
Ranch cowgirls go to Tucson, Vegas, and Hawaii.
Urban cowgirls go to Yellowstone.

TV and movies:
Ranch cowgirls watch *8 Seconds, The Longest Ride, Open Range,* and *True Grit.*
Urban cowgirls watch *Urban Cowboy, Blazing Saddles, 1883,* and *Cowboys & Aliens.*

CHAPTER 12

Livin' the Dream

So, is it cheating to pursue something you aren't?

To pretend you're the
real deal when you're not?

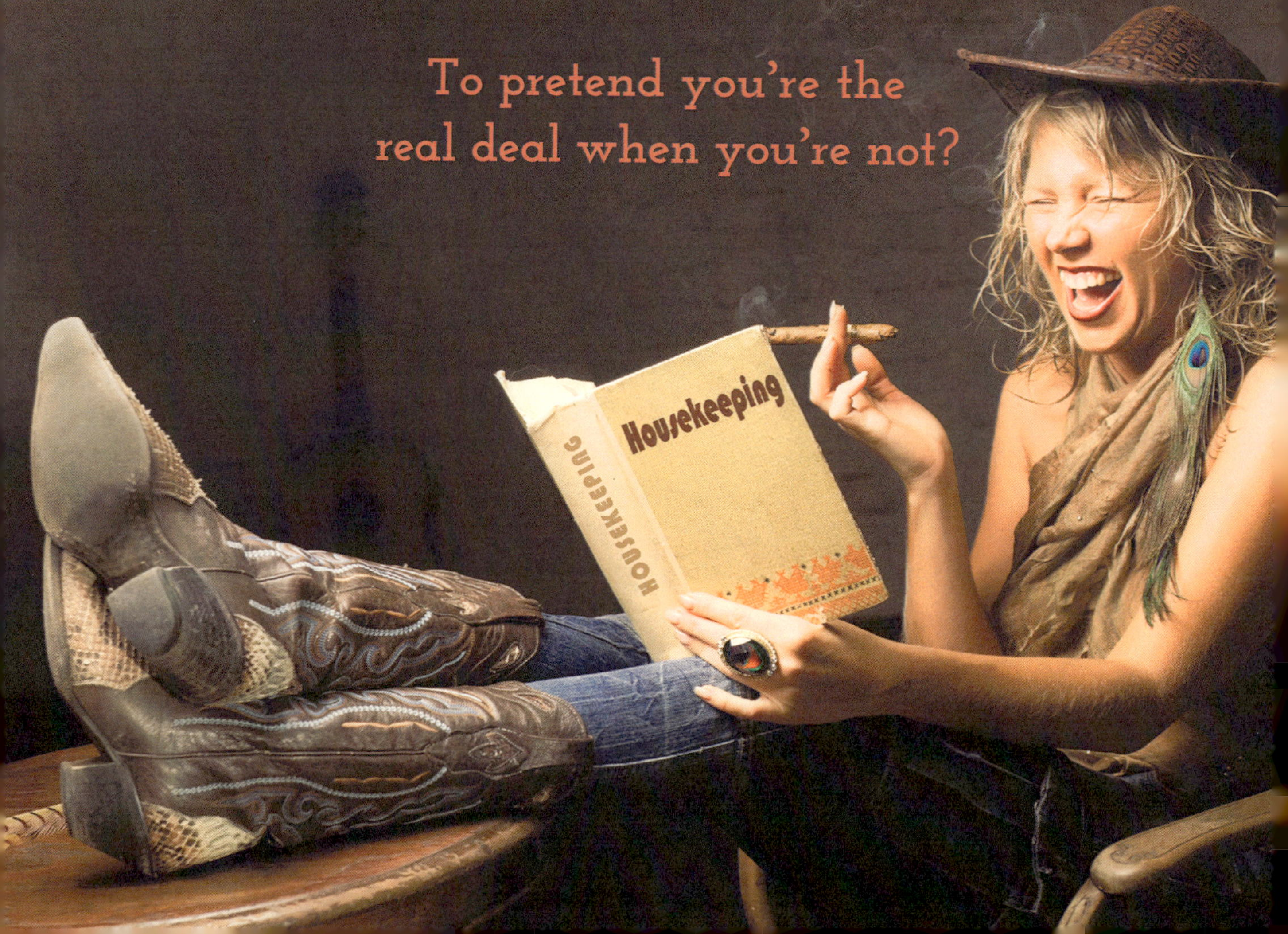

Heck no!

It can be liberating and transforming, especially if it's the female equivalent of America's favorite hero, the cowboy.

Remember:
Every quality bestowed upon real working cowboys, like accountability, courage, compassion, and loyalty, can be applied to women who work the land, ride horses, and stand for American values. *Or just wish they did.*

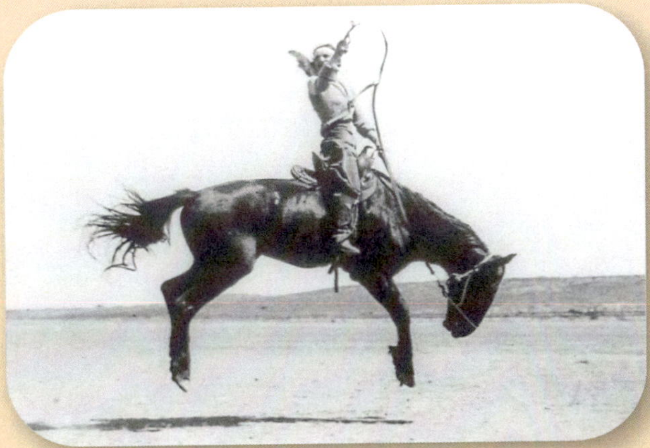

Being a cowgirl means you are powerful, reliable, and committed.

Women in cowboy boots stand taller in every way. They can do everything a cowboy does and look better doing it. Remember, it's not about the clothes or a costume. It's all about heart. You can be an urban cowgirl and protect the Western way of life right where you are.

Be a cowgirl on the inside and you just might change your life!

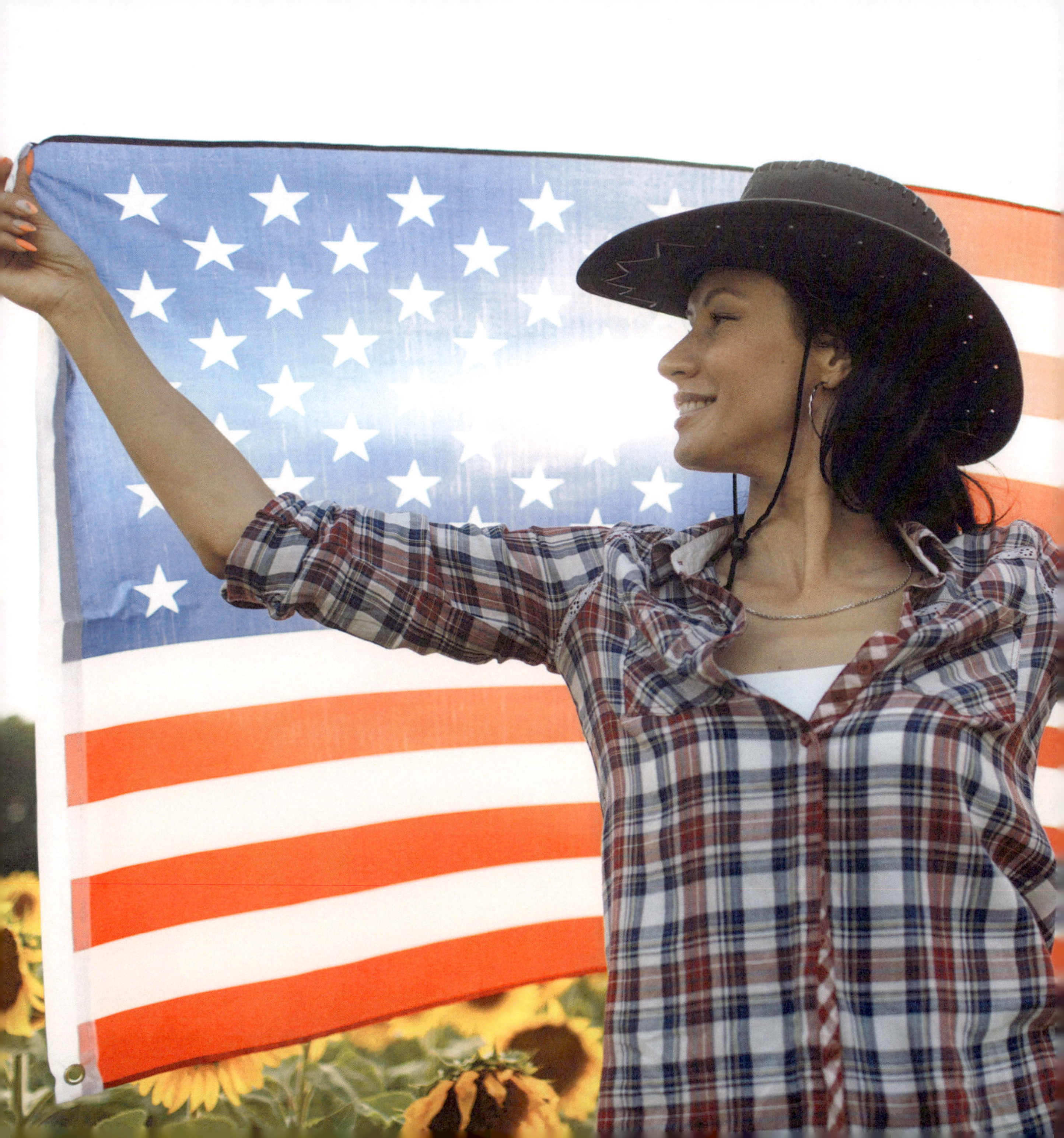

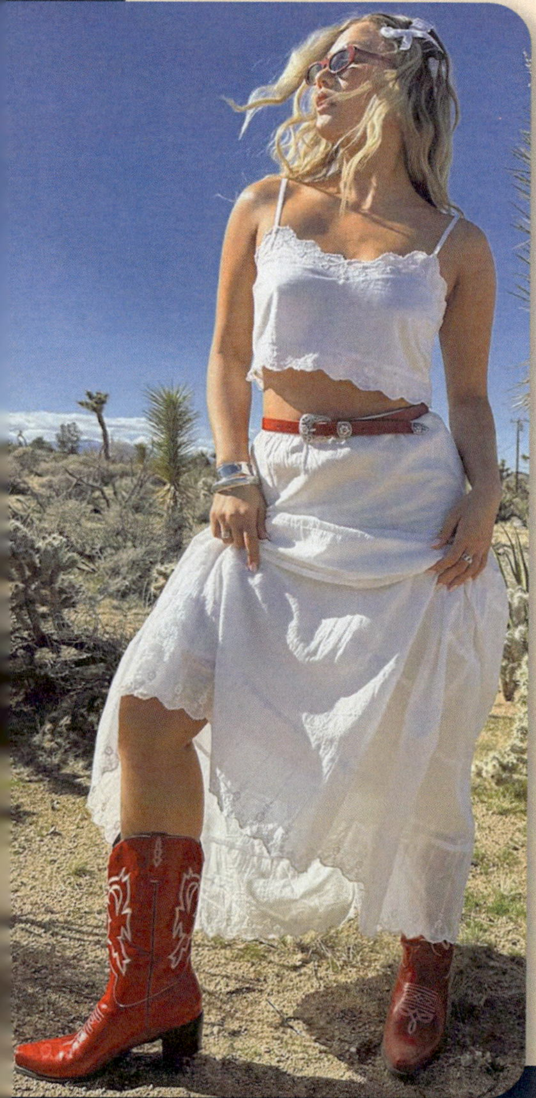

Where to Get the Look

Great stores abound, and these are a few of my favorites, online or in person. Check out vintage dealers too for fun finds from the past!

Mavericks – maverickwesternwear.com

Kowboyz – kowboyz.com

Kemo Sabe – kemosabe.com

Boot Barn – bootbarn.com

Cavender's – cavenders.com

Murdoch's – murdochs.com

Rockabilly Baroness – rockabillybaroness.com

Rockmount Ranchwear – rockmount.com

How to be an Urban Cowgirl is a fun, irreverent guide to understanding the culture everyone loves, ranch hand or not. By now, you can apply what works out there to what works right here. *Cowgirl up!* Soon you'll walk-the-walk and talk-the-talk. With luck, you might even win the heart of a boot-scootin' Romeo. Remember, urban cowgirls can be found in women of every age across the USA. Whether you've ridden a bronc or two (okay, so this isn't your first rodeo), or you're just starting out with your first pair of cowboy boots, this book is advice every city woman can use. Share this little gem for its timeless wisdom and smile appeal.

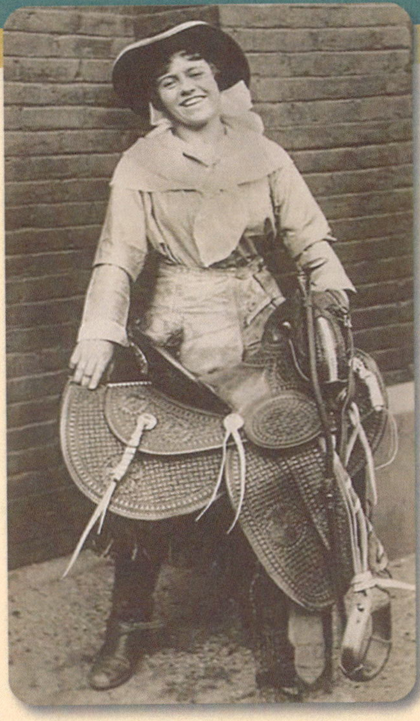

ACKNOWLEDGEMENTS/ SOURCES

Rockmount Ranch Wear
rockmount.com (snapshirt)

Pat Dahnke
patdahnke.com (fringe skirt)

Alltribes
alltribes.com (concho belt)

About the Author

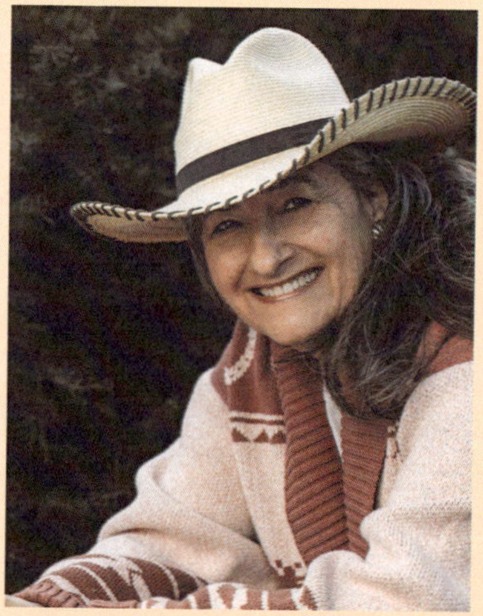

corinnejoybrown.com

Corinne Joy Brown is a Colorado native who has loved the rural Western way of life even though she lives in Denver. She's an award-winning writer about the American West and a journalist who served for 20 years on the staff of *Persimmon Hill*, the magazine of the National Cowboy and Western Heritage Museum in Oklahoma. She has written for *True West Magazine*, *Working Ranch*, *Cowboys & Indians*, *Western & English Today*, *Colorado Life*, and *Western Art & Architecture*. Her last horse, Shamir, passed away, but she still identifies as a cowgirl and always will.

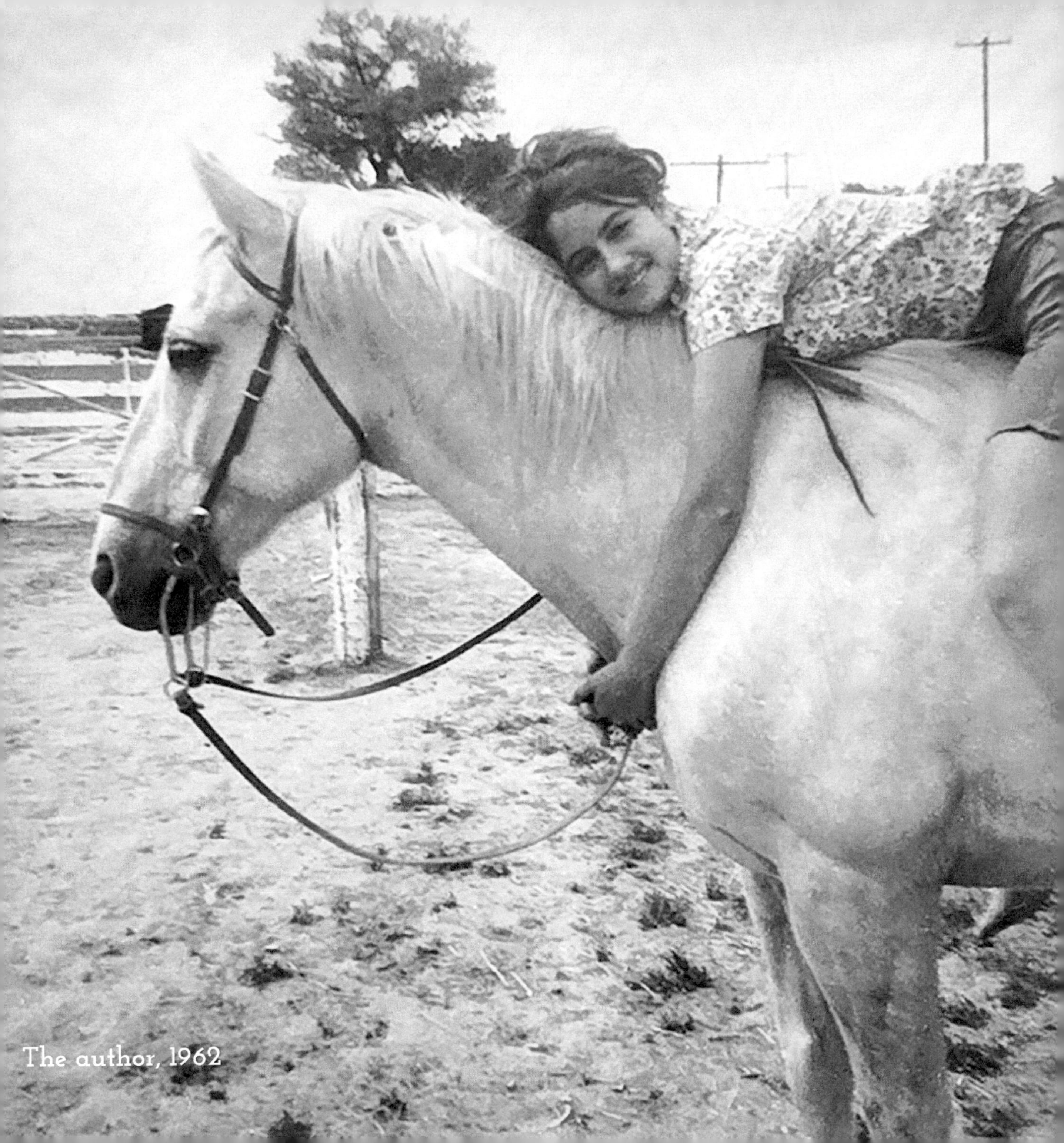

The author, 1962

www.ingramcontent.com/pod-product-compliance
Ingram Content Group UK Ltd.
Pitfield, Milton Keynes, MK11 3LW, UK
UKRC031011310726
14089UKWH00014B/250

* 9 7 8 1 9 6 3 1 1 7 8 3 7 *

9 781963 11783